For Leona:
be free,
go far.

MADE POSSIBLE BY:
My husband, my mother and my father who gave me their fathomless love and steadfast support.

SPECIAL THANKS TO:
Ka Leung Chan and the Hong Kong Cycling Alliance for help with bicycle terminology.

WITH THANKS TO:
David C., Phoebe F., Joyce L., Rachelle L., Jenden L., Minda W., Jenny W., Ruby Y., whose feedback made this book much richer.

Be the first to hear about new Cantonese books!

JOIN THE CATLIKE CLUB:
www.catlikestudio.com/newsletter/

FOLLOW US ON:

 @catlikestudio    @catlikestudiobooks

Tag us with hashtag #mywideandwondrousworld to be featured!

Text and illustrations copyright © Deborah Lau 2022. Icons made by Pixel perfect from www.flaticon.com.
The author/illustrator asserts the moral right to be identified as the author/illustrator of the work.
All rights reserved. First edition published 2022 by Catlike Studio www.catlikestudio.com
Hardcover ISBN: 978-0-6451498-5-2   Paperback ISBN: 978-0-6451498-6-9   eBook ISBN: 978-0-6451498-8-3

我係一個活潑小女孩
ngo5 hai6 jat1 go3 wut6 put3 siu2 neoi5 haai4

我鍾意我嘅奇妙世界
ngo5 zung1 ji3 ngo5 ge3 kei4 miu6 sai3 gaai3

I'm a bright-eyed little girl
I love my wide and wondrous world

我哋一家大細鍾意乜嘢？
ngo5 dei6 jat1 gaa1 daai6 sai3 zung1 ji3 mat1 je5

就係出街一齊踩單車！
zau6 hai6 ceot1 gaai1 jat1 cai4 caai2 daan1 ce1

What does my family like to do?
To go and cycle as a crew!

等我介紹我見過嗰啲喇！
dang2 ngo5 gaai3 siu6 ngo5 gin3 gwo3 go2 di1 laa1

Here's a quick guide to what I've seen tried!

每朝爸爸車我返學
mui5 ziu1 baa1 baa1 ce1 ngo5 faan1 hok6

要上斜路、轉右、再落
jiu1 soeng5 ce3 lou6　　zyun3 jau6　　zoi3 lok6

I've ridden to school with Dad at first light
We go up a big hill then stop to turn right

趕住返工、出去買餸？
gon2 zyu6 faan1 gung1　　ceot1 heoi3 maai5 sung3

If you're going shopping or to work in a hurry?

踩單車就會好輕鬆
caai2 daan1 ce1　zau6　wui5 hou2 hing1 sung1

When you're on a bike, traffic's no worry!

有嘢要搬？又大又重？
jau5　je5　jiu3　bun1　　jau6 daai6　jau6 cung4

Got lots to carry? A big heavy load?

單車運送、好使好用！
daan1 ce1　wan6 sung3　　hou2 sai2 hou2 jung6

Cycling is great, just watch the road!

我試過慢慢上斜
ngo5 si3 gwo3 maan6 maan2 soeng5 ce3

我試過快快落山
ngo5 si3 gwo3 faai3 faai3 lok6 saan1

由日踩到夜
jau4 jat6 caai2 dou3 je6

去邊都好玩
heoi3 bin1 dou1 hou2 waan2

I've cycled up slopes
And zoomed down steep hills
From dawn until dusk
Discovering great thrills

探朋友、食一餐
taam3 pang4 jau5　　sik6　jat1 caan1

去公園、去海灘
heoi3 gung1 jyun4　　heoi3 hoi2 taan1

呢啲活動我已經試咗
ni1　di1　wut6 dung6 ngo5　ji5　ging1　si3　　zo2

剩返一樣我仲未試過……
zing6 faan2 jat1 joeng6 ngo5 zung6 mei6 si3 gwo3

I've visited friends, I've gone out for tea
I've cycled through parks and raced to the sea
I've seen all those places astride on my bike
There's just one more ride that I'd really like...

喺悉尼每年有個日子
hai2 sik1 nei4 mui5 nin4 jau5 go3 jat6 zi2

海港大橋會封路一次……
hoi2 gong2 daai6 kiu4 wui5 fung1 lou6 jat1 ci3

During the spring in Sydney each year
The Harbour Bridge closes and cyclists all cheer...

打招呼、傾偈、睇地圖
daa2　ziu1　fu1　　　king1 gai2　　　tai2　dei6 tou4

一齊排隊預備起步
jat1　cai4 paai4 deoi6 jyu6 bei6 hei2 bou6

We wave, we chat; learn the map by heart
As we line our bikes up at the start

每架單車都唔同
mui5 gaa3 daan1 ce1 dou1 m4 tung4

Every bike is one of a kind

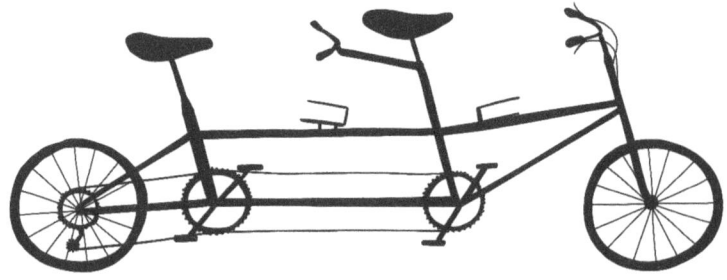

我哋見到幾多種？
ngo5 dei6 gin3 dou3 gei2 do1 zung2

How many types can we find?

有公路車
jau5 gung1 lou6 ce1

There's road bikes

有山地車
jau5 saan1 dei6 ce1

mountain bikes

仲有電動輔助單車
zung6 jau5 din6 dung6 fu6 zo6 daan1 ce1

electric bikes too

邊個踩架載運單車？
bin1 go3 caai2 gaa3 zoi3 wan6 daan1 ce1？

係三個細路同阿爺！
hai6 saam1 go3 sai3 lou6 tung4 aa3 je4

砂石車
saa1 sek6 ce1
Gravel bikes

小輪車
siu2 leon4 ce1
and BMXers;

摺疊車
zip3 dip6 ce1
Folding bikes

梗牙車
gang2 ngaa4 ce1
and fixed gear fixers

有大有細有高有矮
jau5 daai6 jau5 sai3 jau5 gou1 jau5 ai2
Big bikes, small bikes
Short bikes, tall bikes

呢個斜躺車係最古怪
ni1 go3 ce4 tong2 ce1 hai6 zeoi3 gu2 gwaai3

好似瞓低咁樣至去踩
hou2 ci5 fan3 dai1 gam2 joeng2 zi3 heoi3 caai2

And this is the quirkiest bike that's around
To ride a recumbent, you've got to lie down

你估我至鍾意邊款呢？
nei5 gu2 ngo5 zi3 zung1 ji3 bin1 fun2 ne1

梗係我哋嗰架協力車！
gang2 hai6 ngo5 dei6 go2 gaa3 hip3 lik6 ce1

Which is my favorite? Have you guessed?
It's our tandem bike that I like best!

準備，一……二……三，起程！
zeon2 bei6　　jat1　　　　ji6　　　　saam1　　hei2 cing4

一路踩一路睇風景
jat1 lou6 caai2 jat1 lou6 tai2 fung1 ging2

We're off for our Spring Cycle debut
And as we ride, we enjoy the view

清風、藍天、好太陽
cing1 fung1　　nam2 tin1　　hou2 taai3 joeng4

今日十足我夢想
gam1 jat6　sap6　zuk1 ngo5 mung6 soeng2

The spring breeze and the skies of blue
Today is like a dream come true

如果你肯試一試
jyu4 gwo2 nei5 hang2 si3　jat1　si3

我諗你都會鍾意
ngo5 lam2 nei5 dou1 wui5 zung1　ji3

If you're willing, give it a try
I think you'll like it as much as I

ENJOY THIS BOOK?

Please consider leaving a review on Goodreads, Amazon or your book retailer's website.

You can also tag @catlikestudiobooks on Instagram with hashtag #mywideandwondrousworld to be featured!

JOIN THE CATLIKE CLUB

* More Cantonese & bilingual parenting resources
* Recommendations for kids' books
* Early access to our new releases!

Sign up here: www.catlikestudio.com/newsletter/

What would you like to see in our next book?
DM us on Instagram or Facebook and let us know!

 @catlikestudio    @catlikestudiobooks

TONES IN CANTONESE

Tones refer to the relative pitch of your voice when speaking. In English, tones indicate your emotions. In Cantonese, the same sound spoken with a different tone changes the meaning of what is said.

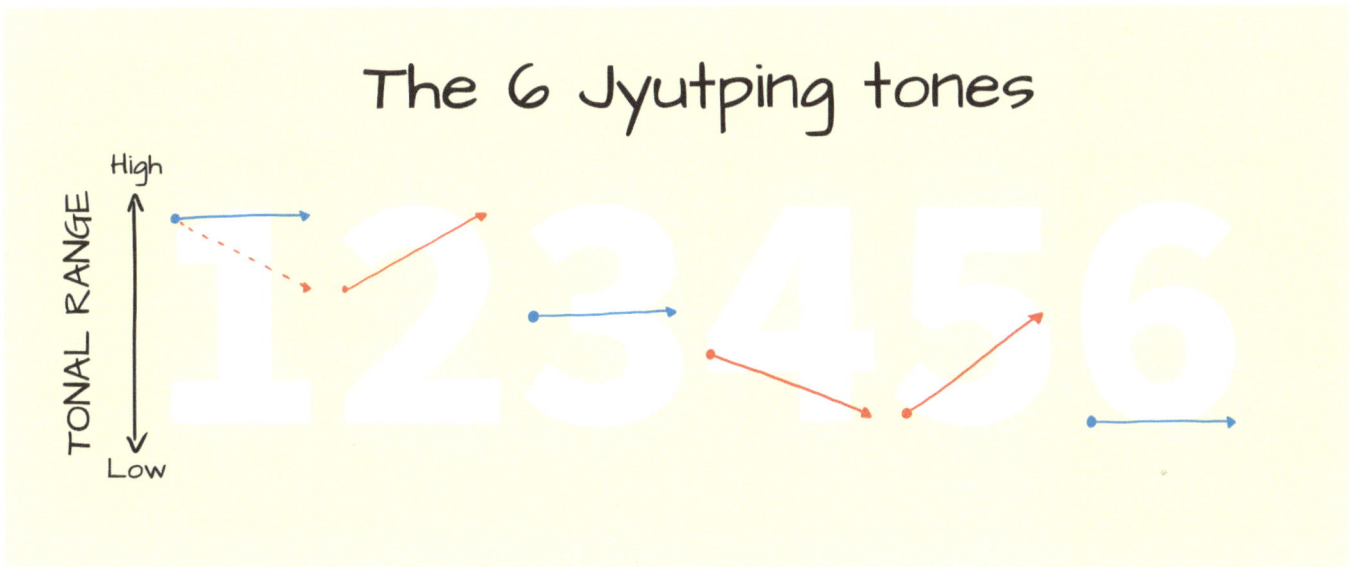

TRANSLATION NOTES

As some artistic liberty was taken to create the bilingual rhymes, the English text is not an exact translation of the Traditional Chinese text. A literal translation is provided on the following pages. Corresponding phrases/words have been color-coded for clarity.

春天踩單車
ceon1 tin1　caai2 daan1 ce1

我係一個活潑小女孩
ngo5 hai6 jat1 go3 wut6 put3 siu2 neoi5 haai4

我鍾意我嘅奇妙世界
ngo5 zung1 ji3 ngo5 ge3 kei4 miu6 sai3 gaai3

我哋一家大細鍾意乜野？
ngo5 dei6 jat1 gaa1 daai6 sai3 zung1 ji3 mat1 je5 ?

就係出街一齊踩單車！
zau6 hai6 ceot1 gaai1 jat1 cai4 caai2 daan1 ce1 !

單車有好多唔同踩法啊
daan1 ce1 jau5 hou2 do1 m4 tung4 caai2 faat3 aa3

等我介紹我見過嘅喇！
dang2 ngo5 gaai3 siu6 ngo5 gin3 gwo3 go2 di1 laa1!

每朝爸爸車我返學
mui5 ziu4 baa1 baa1 ce1 ngo5 faan1 hok6

要上斜路、轉右、再落
jiu1 soeng5 ce3 lou6 , zyun3 jau6 , zoi3 lok6

趕住返工、出去買餸？
gon2 zyu6 faan1 gung1 , ceot1 heoi3 maai5 sung3

踩單車就會好輕鬆！
caai2 daan1 ce1 zau6 wui5 hou2 hing1 sung1 !

有嘢要搬？又大又重？
jau5 je5 jiu3 bun1 ? jau6 daai6 jau6 cung4 ?

單車運送、好使好用！
daan1 ce1 wan6 sung3 , hou2 sai2 hou2 jung6 !

我試過慢慢上斜
ngo5 si3 gwo3 maan6 maan2 soeng5 ce3

我試過快快落山
ngo5 si3 gwo3 faai3 faai3 lok6 saan1

由日踩到夜
jau4 jat6 caai2 dou3 je6

去邊都好玩
heoi3 bin1 dou1 hou2 waan2

I am one bright-eyed little girl

I like my wonderful world

What does my family enjoy?

Going out to ride bikes together

There are many ways to ride bicycles

Let me introduce the ones I have seen

Every morning Daddy takes me to school

Up a sloping road, turn right, and down

In a rush to go to work, go to buy food?

Cycling is very relaxing

Got things to move? Is it heavy and big?

Bicycle transportation is very useful

I have slowly gone up slopes

I have quickly gone down hills

Cycling from day time until night time

Having fun wherever I go

探朋友、食一餐
taam3 pang4 jau5 , sik6 jat1 caan1

去公園、去海灘
heoi3 gung1 jyun4 , heoi3 hoi2 taan1

呢啲活動我已經試咗
ni1 di1 wut6 dung6 ngo5 ji5 ging1 si3 zo2

剩返一樣我仲未試過⋯⋯
zing6 faan2 jat1 joeng6 ngo5 zung6 mei6 si3 gwo3

喺悉尼每年有個日子
hai2 sik1 nei4 mui5 nin4 jau5 go3 jat6 zi2

海港大橋會封路一次⋯⋯
hoi2 gong2 daai6 kiu4 wui5 fung1 lou6 jat1 ci3

去到我慢慢周圍望
heoi3 dou3 ngo5 maan6 maan2 zau1 wai4 mong6

咁多人好熱鬧好忙
gam3 do1 jan4 hou2 jit6 naau6 hou2 mong4

打招呼、傾偈、睇地圖
daa2 ziu1 fu1 , king1 gai2 , tai2 dei6 tou4

一齊排隊預備起步
jat1 cai4 paai4 deoi6 jyu6 bei6 hei2 bou6

每架單車都唔同
mui5 gaa3 daan1 ce1 dou1 m4 tung4

我哋見到幾多種？
ngo5 dei6 gin3 dou3 gei2 do1 zung2 ?

有公路車、有山地車、
jau5 gung1 lou6 ce1 , jau5 saan1 dei6 ce1 ,

仲有電動輔助單車
zung6 jau5 din6 dung6 fu6 zo6 daan1 ce1

邊個踩㗎載運單車？
bin1 go3 caai2 gaa2 zoi3 wan6 daan1 ce1 ?

係三個細路同阿爺
hai6 saam1 go3 sai3 lou6 tung4 aa3 je4

Cycling in Spring

(a literal translation from Traditional Chinese to English)

Visit friends, eat one meal

Go to the park, go to the beach

I have already tried these activities

There is one thing I have not tried yet…

In Sydney each year there is a date

The Harbor Bridge will close once

On arrival I slowly look around

With so many people, it's lively and busy

We greet, chat, look at the map

We line up together and wait to begin

Every bike is different

How many kinds can we see?

There's road bikes, there's mountain bikes

And also electric bikes

Who's that riding the cargo bike?

It is three kids and their grandpa!

砂石車、小輪車、
saa1 sek6 ce1、siu2 leon4 ce1、

摺疊車、梗牙車、
zip3 dip6 ce1、gang2 ngaa4 ce1、

有大有細
jau5 daai6 jau5 sai3

有高有矮
jau5 gou1 jau5 ai2

呢個斜躺車係最古怪
ni1 go3 ce4 tong2 ce1 hai6 zeoi3 gu2 gwaai3

好似瞓低咁樣至去踩
hou2 ci5 fan3 dai1 gam3 joeng6 zi3 heoi3 caai2

你估我至鍾意邊款呢？
nei5 gu2 ngo5 zi3 zung1 ji3 bin1 fun2 ne1？

梗係我哋嗰嚟協力車！
gang2 hai6 ngo5 dei6 go2 gaa2 hip3 lik6 ce1！

準備，一……二……三，起程！
zeon2 bei6，jat1……ji6……saam1，hei2 cing4！

一路踩一路睇風景
jat1 lou6 caai2 jat1 lou6 tai2 fung1 ging2

清風、藍天、好太陽
cing1 fung1、laam4 tin1、hou2 taai3 joeng4

今日十足我夢想
gam1 jat6 sap6 zuk1 ngo5 mung6 soeng2

如果你肯試一試
jyu4 gwo2 nei5 hang2 si3 jat1 si3

我諗你都會鍾意
ngo5 lam2 nei5 dou1 wui5 zung1 ji3

Gravel bikes, BMX bikes,

Folding bikes, fixed gear bikes,

There are big, there are small

There are tall, there are short

This recumbent bike is the strangest

You can lie down to ride it

Guess which kind I like best?

Our tandem bike of course!

Ready, one…two…three, go!

As we ride, we look at the scenery

Fresh breeze, blue sky, sunny

Today is just like my dream

If you are willing to give it a try

I think you will enjoy it too

For help with pronounciation, visit www.catlikestudio.com/readalong/ for a FREE audio book in Cantonese and English!

Lightning Source UK Ltd.
Milton Keynes UK
UKHW050836310322
400863UK00002B/23